San Francisco
IN THE 1850s

San Francisco
IN THE 1850s

33 PHOTOGRAPHIC VIEWS BY
G. R. FARDON

WITH AN INTRODUCTION BY
ROBERT A. SOBIESZEK

The International Museum of Photography
At George Eastman House, Rochester and
DOVER PUBLICATIONS, INC., NEW YORK

Published in Canada by General Publishing Company, Ltd., 30 Lesmill Road, Don Mills, Toronto, Ontario.
Published in the United Kingdom by Constable and Company, Ltd., 10 Orange Street, London WC2H 7EG.

This Dover edition, first published in 1977, is an unabridged republication of the work first published by Herre & Bauer, at the Office of the San Francisco *Journal*, 66 Merchant Street, San Francisco, in 1856 under the title *San Francisco Album. Photographs of the Most Beautiful Views and Public Buildings of San Francisco*. A new Introduction has been written especially for the present edition by Robert A. Sobieszek, and captions based on the original "Index" have been added to the picture pages.

International Standard Book Number: 0-486-23459-2
Library of Congress Catalog Card Number: 76-48591

Manufactured in the United States of America
Dover Publications, Inc.
180 Varick Street
New York, N.Y. 10014

INTRODUCTION

In the pictorial and graphic arts, the nineteenth century exhibited a penchant for the encyclopedic recording of just about everything. The images of peoples and races, architecture and landscapes, machinery and works of art were all pictured, collected and studied. Much of this activity took place in the newly flourishing urban centers. In fact, these new urban landscapes became themselves the subjects for the draftsman, engraver, painter and, after 1839, the photographer. Some of the earliest existing photographs show us the look of such cities as London, Paris and Berlin. These cities grew along with photography, and the photograph kept abreast of the need to record the continual changes taking place in them.

Photography has an incredible facility to furnish a viewing public with vast quantities of images. In a much shorter time and with much less physical effort than painting, photography can record not just a quintessential scene, but literally hundreds of equally representative views which together form a much more complete record of facts. Throughout the last century the camera was frequently inducted into the service of pictorial artists to document large tracts of the urban landscape and to catalog areas that were being planned for urban renewal.

In the nineteenth century major cities were in many regards symbols of nationalistic progress. Haussmann's grand boulevards streaming through Paris signified modernization and progress, as did the tearing down of the Glasgow closes and slums. Urban renewal was not especially crucial in the younger cities of America. New York, Philadelphia, Washington and Boston, among others, were all well documented by photographers; so much so that we can today trace their development clearly through these vintage photographs. Of all the major American cities of that century, none were as frequently and thoroughly photographed as was one of the youngest urban centers—San Francisco. Per-

haps it was so often photographed because it represented so many of the dreams of young America—the Westward expansion, the laissez-faire social structure of the frontier and the potential for immediate wealth in the gold fields of 1849. San Francisco entered into the modern world with the discovery of gold in California, exactly a decade after the invention of photography. By 1849, photography, in the form of the daguerreotype, had progressed enough to be fairly convenient and relatively reliable. Along with the gold prospectors and merchant princes, a number of daguerreotypists emigrated into the Bay City and began documenting its appearance up to the Great Fire of 1851 and after its efficiently swift reconstruction. A fair number of large, multiple-plate panoramas of San Francisco made between 1850 and 1852 still exist. While they are brilliantly detailed and exquisitely crafted, they all possess the one serious limitation that they were and are unique images. Relatively few were able to see them and appreciate the wonders of the city. Comparatively, many more learned what the city looked like from Charles Méryon's etching and drypoint of 1856, copied from just such a daguerreotype panorama. The ability to publish and disseminate photographic views was both necessary and desired; it had to wait for the practical advent of paper photographs, printed from negatives, to allow for such dissemination.

One of the earliest photographers to experiment commercially with this method for wider popular distribution of his pictures was George Robinson Fardon. Born in England in 1806, he arrived in San Francisco at the age of 43. He is credited with introducing the wet collodion process during his ten years there. In 1859 he moved to Victoria, British Columbia, where, after a two-year respite, he continued his photographic activities until the early 1870s. He acted as an agent for Langley & Co. until his death in Victoria on August 19, 1886. For additional information, see Ralph Greenhill's *Early Photography in Canada,* Oxford University Press, Toronto, 1965.

G. R. Fardon's *San Francisco Album. Photographs of the Most Beautiful Views and Public Buildings of San Francisco* is important as an American publication for a number of reasons. It is the first *published* compilation of photographs of any American city. Published only seven years after the '49 gold rush, Fardon's book had the potential for spreading images of the city's appearance to a great many more people than a set of daguerreotype plates could have. More importantly in some ways, Fardon's *San Francisco Album* was a more telling portrait of the city than any previously issued set of plates had been. Not only did the photographer include in his group of 33 shots general views of the city from vantage points such as Rincon Point and Telegraph Hill, but he added to these some rather sensitive renderings of the major buildings and avenues such as Montgomery Street, City Hall and the Merchants' Exchange—all quite famous in Californian history. Furthermore, Fardon shows the viewer what Alcatras [sic] Island, the "Los Dolores" Mission and the Orphans' Asylum looked like in 1856. As an item of Californian incunabula, the Fardon album is of major significance.

The *San Francisco Album* is also somewhat problematic in both its origins and present states. We know that the work was published by Herre & Bauer in conjunction with the San Francisco *Journal,* and that is about all. Few copies of the *San Francisco Album* seem to be extant, two in public collections: the International Museum of Photography in Rochester, New York, and The Huntington Library in San Marino, California. The exact size of the edition is not recorded in any locatable source, so it is uncertain just how useful a means of visual dissemination the work was. What we do know is that the album is one of the earliest existing series of views of any American or European city. The photographs were most likely made on glass-plate negatives using the recently developed wet collodion process (1851), and printed on albumen printing paper whose emulsion consisted chiefly of egg whites and silver chloride. The Fardon album is an invaluable source of visual fact about one of America's most colorful and beautiful cities in its infancy, captured by a visual artist sensitive to the look and to the nuances of San Francisco.

I would like to thank the Provincial Archives of British Columbia and Wendy van Oldenborgh of New Westminster, B.C., for their help in collecting the above biographical data.

ROBERT A. SOBIESZEK
Associate Curator, Photography
International Museum of Photography
Rochester, New York

SAN FRANCISCO ALBUM.

PHOTOGRAPHS

OF THE MOST BEAUTIFUL

VIEWS AND PUBLIC BUILDINGS

OF

SAN FRANCISCO.

Photographed by G. R. FARDON.

PUBLISHED BY

HERRE & BAUER,

AT THE OFFICE OF THE SAN FRANCISCO JOURNAL,
66 MERCHANT STREET.

INDEX.

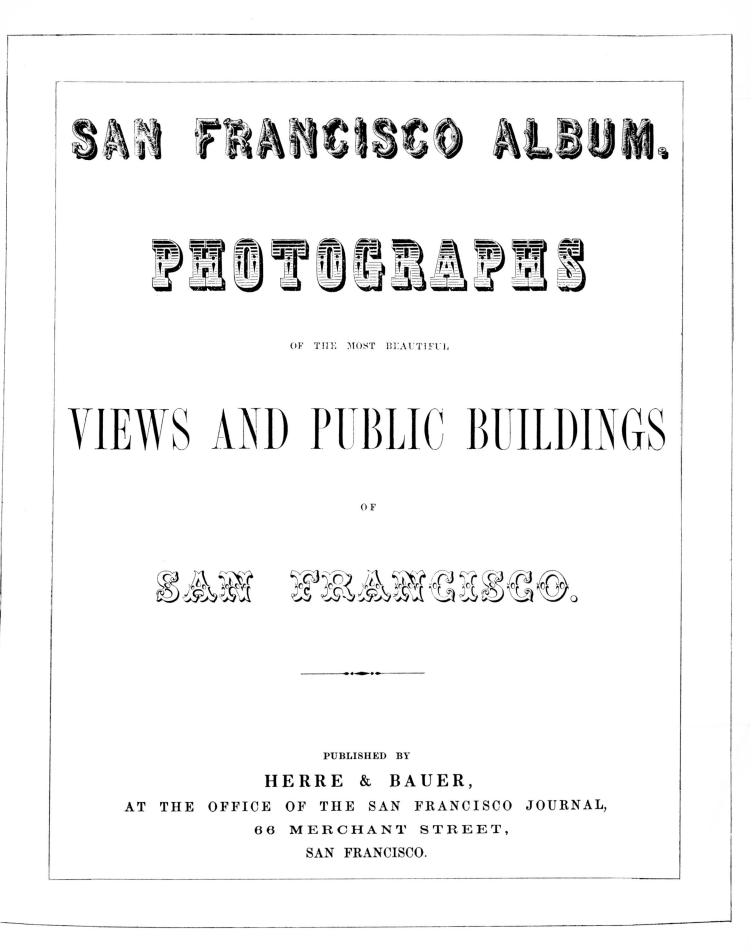

SAN FRANCISCO ALBUM.

PHOTOGRAPHS

OF THE MOST BEAUTIFUL

VIEWS AND PUBLIC BUILDINGS

OF

SAN FRANCISCO.

PUBLISHED BY

HERRE & BAUER,

AT THE OFFICE OF THE SAN FRANCISCO JOURNAL,

66 MERCHANT STREET,

SAN FRANCISCO.

1. Telegraph Hill, taken from the corner of Stockton and Sacramento Streets.

2.   Monumental Engine house, on the Plaza.

3.   Merchants' Exchange, on Battery Street.

4. Former Post Office, the rally of the "Law and Order" Party.

5. View of the City from Stockton Street, containing the portions between Washington and Sacramento Streets.

6. The Cathedral (St. Mary's Church).

7. City Hall.

8. Fort Vigilance.

9. View down Sacramento Street.

10. The Custom House.

11. View of the west side of Montgomery Street, from Washington to Pacific.

12.   (A) St. Francis' Hook and Ladder No. 1.

12.   (B) Knickerbocker Engine House No. 5.

13. View over the City, containing portions between California and Bush Streets.

13

14. View over Happy Valley.

15. Montgomery Block, Montgomery Street.

16. View down Stockton Street.

17. North side of Montgomery Street, from California to Sacramento.

18. View of North Beach, from Telegraph Hill.

19. Kearny Street.

20. East side of Montgomery Street.

21. View over the City from Harrison Street.

22. View from Rincon Point.

23. South Park.

24. View of Russian Hill [this section now known as Nob Hill] from Telegraph Hill.

25. View over the Plaza.

26. Alcatras Island.

27. Battery Street.

28. California Street.

29. View from Kearny Street—in the foreground the Orphans' Asylum.

30.   Mission of "Los Dolores."

[Unidentified view, not listed in original index.]